LIVE IT:
PERSEVERANCE

KYLIE BURNS

Crabtree Publishing Company
www.crabtreebooks.com

Author: Kylie Burns
Coordinating editor: Bonnie Dobkin
Publishing plan research and development:
  Sean Charlebois, Reagan Miller
  Crabtree Publishing Company
Editor: Reagan Miller
Proofreader: Crystal Sikkens
Editorial director: Kathy Middleton
Production coordinator: Margaret Salter
Prepress technician: Margaret Salter

Logo design: Samantha Crabtree
Project Manager: Santosh Vasudevan (Q2AMEDIA)
Art Direction: Rahul Dhiman (Q2AMEDIA)
Design: Neha Kaul and Niyati Gosain (Q2AMEDIA)
Illustrations: Q2AMEDIA
Front Cover: After other scientists had given up and after many attempts of his own, Thomas Edison, one of the world's greatest inventors, finally invented the electric light bulb.
Title Page: Surfer Bethany Hamilton survived a horrific shark attack and got back into surfing after losing her arm.

Library and Archives Canada Cataloguing in Publication

Burns, Kylie
      Live it: perseverance / Kylie Burns.

(Crabtree character sketches)
Includes index.
ISBN 978-0-7787-4884-7 (bound).--ISBN 978-0-7787-4917-2 (pbk.)

      1. Perseverance (Ethics)--Juvenile literature. 2. Biography--Juvenile
literature. I. Title. II. Title: Perseverance. III. Series: Crabtree character
sketches

BJ1533.P4B87 2010   j179'.9   C2009-905514-7

Library of Congress Cataloging-in-Publication Data

Burns, Kylie.
  Live it. Perseverance / Kylie Burns.
      p. cm. -- (Crabtree character sketches)
  Includes index.
  ISBN 978-0-7787-4917-2 (pbk. : alk. paper) -- ISBN 978-0-7787-4884-7 (reinforced library binding : alk. paper)
  1. Perseverance (Ethics)--Juvenile literature. 2. Conduct of life--Juvenile literature. I. Title. II. Title: Perserverance. III. Series.

BJ1533.P4B87 2010
179'.9--dc22
                                              2009036787

Crabtree Publishing Company

Printed in the USA/122009/BG20090930

www.crabtreebooks.com   1-800-387-7650

Published in Canada
Crabtree Publishing
616 Welland Ave.
St. Catharines, ON
L2M 5V6

Published in the United States
Crabtree Publishing
PMB 59051
350 Fifth Avenue, 59th Floor
New York, New York 10118

Published in the United Kingdom
Crabtree Publishing
Maritime House
Basin Road North, Hove
BN41 1WR

Published in Australia
Crabtree Publishing
386 Mt. Alexander Rd.
Ascot Vale (Melbourne)
VIC 3032

CONTENTS

WHAT IS PERSEVERANCE?

PERSEVERANCE MEANS ALWAYS TRYING, EVEN WHEN THINGS ARE REALLY HARD. THE PEOPLE YOU WILL READ ABOUT IN THIS BOOK FACED DIFFICULT CHALLENGES, BUT THEY NEVER GAVE UP. GET READY FOR SIX AMAZING STORIES!

BETHANY HAMILTON
TEENAGE SURFING CHAMPION

SHANIA TWAIN
SINGER AND SONGWRITER

DR. ROBERT BALLARD
OCEANOGRAPHER WHO DISCOVERED THE REMAINS OF THE TITANIC

ANNE SULLIVAN AND HELEN KELLER
A TEACHER OF THE DEAF AND HER STUDENT

WILMA RUDOLPH
POLIO SURVIVOR AND OLYMPIC CHAMPION

THOMAS EDISON
SCIENTIST AND INVENTOR

PERSEVERANCE AFTER AN ACCIDENT

BETHANY HAMILTON

WHO IS SHE?
SURFING CHAMPION, BEST-SELLING AUTHOR, AND *INSPIRATIONAL* SPEAKER

WHY HER?
SHE RETURNED TO SURFING AFTER LOSING HER ARM IN A HORRIBLE ACCIDENT

BETHANY HAMILTON WAS JUST 13 YEARS OLD WHEN SHE WAS ATTACKED BY A 14-FOOT TIGER SHARK*. NOT ONLY DID BETHANY SURVIVE, SHE SHOCKED THE WORLD WITH HER DECISION TO RETURN TO SURFING!

LET'S LOOK AT HOW BETHANY'S INCREDIBLE PERSEVERANCE HELPED HER GET BACK ON HER BOARD.

*ABOUT 4.3 METERS

BETHANY HAMILTON BECAME A SURFING CHAMPION WHEN SHE WAS JUST EIGHT YEARS OLD.

ONE OF OUR BRIGHTEST NEW STARS IS TODAY'S CHAMPION IN NOT ONE, BUT TWO EVENTS. LET'S HEAR IT FOR THE AMAZING BETHANY HAMILTON!

CONGRATULATIONS, BETHANY, ON WINNING TWO EVENTS. WHAT ARE YOUR DREAMS FOR THE FUTURE?

I'M GOING TO BE A PROFESSIONAL SURFER! I WANT TO SURF ALL OVER THE WORLD!

IT WAS HARD, BUT BETHANY KEPT TRYING TO GET UP ON HER BOARD AND CATCH A WAVE. THE CROWD BEGAN TO CHEER HER ON.

YOU CAN DO IT!

C'MON BETHANY, KEEP TRYING!

AMAZINGLY, BETHANY SOON MANAGED TO GET UP ON HER BOARD AND RIDE THE WAVES!

HOORAY!

THAT'S AMAZING!

WAY TO GO, BETHANY!

IN 2004, BETHANY WON THE ESPY AWARD FOR "BEST COMEBACK ATHLETE OF THE YEAR."

CONGRATULATIONS, BETHANY. NO ONE DESERVES THIS MORE!

ESPY

BETHANY SHOWED PERSEVERANCE WHEN SHE PUSHED PAST HER FEARS AND RETURNED TO SURFING. DO YOU THINK YOU WOULD HAVE BEEN AS DETERMINED AS SHE WAS? NOW'S YOUR CHANCE TO FIND OUT!

WHAT WOULD YOU DO?

YOU LOVE TO GO MOUNTAIN BIKING WITH FRIENDS, BUT ONE DAY YOU'RE ON A PATH THAT'S A LOT ROUGHER THAN USUAL. YOUR BIKE HITS A ROCK, AND YOU FLIP OVER, BREAKING YOUR RIGHT ARM AND COLLARBONE. IT TAKES YOU WEEKS TO RECOVER, AND YOU'RE IN A LOT OF PAIN.

LATER THAT SUMMER, YOUR FRIENDS PLAN ANOTHER BIKE TRIP, IN THE SAME AREA. NO ONE'S PUSHING YOU TO JOIN THEM BUT YOU KNOW YOU'RE INVITED. WHAT WOULD YOU DO?

SHANIA TWAIN

WHO IS SHE?
A FAMOUS SINGER AND SONGWRITER

WHY HER?
SHANIA NEVER LOST HOPE, EVEN WHEN A TRAGIC ACCIDENT THREATENED TO DESTROY HER DREAMS.

SHANIA TWAIN WENT FROM SMALL-TOWN GIRL TO SUPERSTAR OF THE MUSIC WORLD.

THERE WERE CHALLENGES ALONG THE WAY, BUT PERSEVERANCE GOT HER THROUGH. LET'S SEE HOW.

SHANIA TWAIN WAS BORN IN WINDSOR, ONTARIO. SHE WAS THE SECOND OF THREE GIRLS. HER DAD LEFT HOME AFTER THE YOUNGEST WAS BORN.

SOMETIMES I JUST DON'T KNOW HOW WE CAN KEEP GOING, MAYBE IT'S TIME FOR A NEW START.

EVENTUALLY THE FAMILY MOVED TO A TOWN CALLED TIMMINS. FOUR YEARS LATER, SHANIA'S MOTHER MET AND MARRIED A **FORESTER** NAMED JERRY TWAIN.

GIDDY-UP, HORSEY!

WHEEEE!

JERRY'S SUCH A GREAT FATHER.

SHANIA'S PARENTS EVENTUALLY ADDED TWO MORE CHILDREN—SONS—TO THEIR HAPPY FAMILY. THERE WAS PLENTY OF LOVE, BUT VERY LITTLE MONEY.

A MUSTARD SANDWICH AGAIN? HERE—I'LL SHARE SOME OF MY LUNCH WITH YOU.

SHHH... IF THE TEACHER HEARS YOU, SHE'LL KNOW WE'RE POOR AND THEY'LL TRY TO TAKE ME AWAY FROM MY PARENTS. REMEMBER WHAT HAPPENED TO THAT BOY IN OUR CLASS LAST YEAR?

DESPITE HER SITUATION, THERE WAS ONE THING THAT ALWAYS MADE SHANIA FEEL GOOD.

I DON'T WANT TO SHOP ANYMORE. LET'S GO IN THERE AND GET A SODA!

GET A SODA? YOU'RE JUST GOING TO WASTE YOUR MONEY SINGING ALONG WITH THE JUKEBOX AGAIN!

BUT SHANIA COULDN'T BE STOPPED. ALL SHE WANTED TO DO WAS SING.

I'M JUST A POOR GIRL FROM THE COUNTRY...

SOON, SHANIA'S MOTHER BEGAN TO ARRANGE SINGING *OPPORTUNITIES* FOR SHANIA IN THE COMMUNITY. JERRY TAUGHT SHANIA TO PLAY THE GUITAR.

country's finest

THE CROWD LOVES HER, JERRY!

I'D SAY SO... I THINK SHE'S ON HER WAY!

11

AFTER HIGH SCHOOL, SHANIA MOVED TO TORONTO TO SEEK SUCCESS AS A SINGER.

THANK YOU! GOOD NIGHT!

GLAD TO HAVE YOU HOME, HONEY. SOON YOU'LL BE A FAMOUS SINGER TOURING THE WORLD!

BUT I'LL ALWAYS MAKE TIME FOR MY FAMILY!

IN THE SUMMER, SHE WORKED FOR JERRY, PLANTING TREES ACROSS NORTHERN ONTARIO.

SADLY, IN THE FALL OF 1987, SHANIA'S FAMILY SUFFERED A SHOCKING LOSS.

I'M VERY SORRY. NEITHER OF YOUR PARENTS SURVIVED THE CAR ACCIDENT.

I CAN'T BELIEVE THIS... IT MUST BE A MISTAKE.

JUST 21 YEARS OLD, SHANIA GAVE UP HER BIG-CITY LIFE AND TOOK ON THE ROLE OF CAREGIVER FOR HER YOUNGER SISTER AND BROTHERS.

WHY DO WE HAVE TO MOVE? I DON'T WANT TO LEAVE MY FRIENDS.

THE ONLY JOB I COULD FIND IS AT A RESORT 300 MILES* AWAY—SO KEEP PACKING!

*ABOUT 483 KILOMETERS

PERSEVERANCE IN A QUEST

DR. ROBERT BALLARD

WHO IS HE?
AN OCEAN SCIENTIST AND EXPLORER

WHY HIM?
DR. BALLARD MADE ONE OF THE MOST AMAZING DISCOVERIES OF ALL TIME—HE LOCATED THE WRECK OF THE *TITANIC!*

AS A BOY, ROBERT BALLARD DREAMED OF EXPLORING THE OCEAN. HE MADE THAT DREAM COME TRUE, BUT HIS DREAM OF FINDING THE *TITANIC* WOULD PROVE TO BE MUCH MORE CHALLENGING.

READ ON TO FIND OUT HOW PERSEVERANCE HELPED DR. BALLARD SUCCEED IN THE GREATEST *QUEST* OF HIS CAREER.

ON APRIL 14, 1912, THE MIGHTY SHIP *TITANIC* STRUCK AN ICEBERG AND SANK TO THE BOTTOM OF THE ATLANTIC OCEAN. THE SHIP'S FINAL RESTING PLACE REMAINED A MYSTERY FOR THE NEXT 73 YEARS.

THEN ROBERT BALLARD TOOK AN INTEREST.

ROBERT BALLARD BEGAN HIS CAREER AS A **MARINE GEOLOGIST** IN THE NAVY. LATER, IN THE NAVY RESERVE, HE WORKED AT THE WOODS HOLE OCEANOGRAPHIC INSTITUTE.

HEY, BALLARD, LOOK AT THOSE TUBES NEAR THE HOT SPRINGS!

THOSE AREN'T TUBES—THEY'RE GIANT WORMS! THEY MUST BE 8 FEET* LONG!

*ABOUT 2.4 METERS

IN 1973, BALLARD BECAME FRUSTRATED WITH THE LACK OF FUNDING FOR HIS PROJECTS.

I AGREE. BUT HOW DO WE GET WHAT WE NEED?

WE NEED MORE MONEY TO IMPROVE OUR EQUIPMENT AND DO THE RIGHT KIND OF RESEARCH.

WE HAVE TO COME UP WITH SOMETHING THAT WILL EXCITE PEOPLE, SOMETHING LIKE... FINDING THE *TITANIC*!

BALLARD'S IDEA WAS GREAT FOR RAISING MONEY. OVER THE YEARS, HE BECAME MORE AND MORE FASCINATED BY THE *TITANIC* ITSELF.

THANKS FOR MEETING WITH ME, MR. TANTUM. I'M TOLD YOUR NICKNAME IS "MR. *TITANIC*!"

CALL ME BILL. YES, THE *TITANIC* FASCINATES ME—IT'S THE GREATEST OF ALL SEA DISASTERS. LET ME TELL YOU WHAT I KNOW...

BY 1977, BALLARD HAD RAISED ENOUGH MONEY TO SUPPORT A 12-DAY **EXPEDITION**. HE USED A BORROWED SHIP AND BORROWED EQUIPMENT. BUT JUST AS THE MISSION GOT UNDERWAY...

WATCH OUT! IT'S BREAKING!

I'LL NEVER GET FUNDING AFTER THIS!

15

BALLARD RETURNED TO HIS RESEARCH, BUT THE *TITANIC* WAS NEVER FAR FROM HIS MIND. THEN, IN 1981...

"TEXAS MILLIONAIRE JACK GRIMM HAS ANNOUNCED HIS PLANS TO LOCATE THE LOST WRECKAGE OF THE *TITANIC*..." NO. THAT DISCOVERY SHOULD BE MINE!

The Boston Globe

MISSION TITANIC!

BUT GRIMM HAD NO SUCCESS.

BALLARD'S HOPES OF FINDING THE *TITANIC* WERE IGNITED AGAIN. BY 1985, HE HAD DEVELOPED A NEW UNDERWATER ROBOT CRAFT CALLED THE *ARGO*. HE AND HIS TEAM WENT BACK TO SEA. AT FIRST, THEY HAD NO LUCK.

TIME'S RUNNING OUT, ROBERT. WHAT DO YOU WANT TO DO?

LET'S GET THE *ARGO* IN THE WATER. KEEP AN EYE OUT FOR SHIP *DEBRIS*. IT COULD LEAD US TO THE *TITANIC*.

THE *ARGO* WAS LOWERED ON A CABLE AND BEGAN *TRANSMITTING* VIDEO IMAGES FROM THE OCEAN FLOOR.

WE ONLY HAVE FIVE DAYS LEFT, AND WE HAVEN'T SEEN ANYTHING OTHER THAN SEA SLUG TRAILS!

TELL ME ABOUT IT! I THINK MY EYES ARE GOING TO FALL OUT! BALLARD'S GOING TO HAVE TO GIVE UP.

BUT THEIR LUCK WAS ABOUT TO CHANGE.

WHAT IS IT? STU, WHAT DO YOU SEE?

IT'S—I THINK IT'S A **BOILER FURNACE.** THIS IS IT! GO GET BALLARD!

THE UNDERWATER CAMERA HAD LOCATED THE FIRST PIECE OF THE *TITANIC* **WRECKAGE.** BALLARD AND HIS CREW WERE ECSTATIC!

SOON, THE *TITANIC* ITSELF CAME INTO VIEW. BALLARD'S LONGTIME DREAM HAD FINALLY COME TRUE!

IT HAS TAKEN **12** YEARS... BUT THERE SHE IS.

IT WAS ALMOST **2:00** AM—CLOSE TO THE SAME TIME THAT THE *TITANIC* WENT DOWN ON THAT FATEFUL NIGHT **73** YEARS AGO.

DR. ROBERT BALLARD NEVER GAVE UP, EVEN WHEN HIS EQUIPMENT FAILED... OR TIME WAS RUNNING OUT... OR WHEN NO ONE BELIEVED IN HIM. WHAT WOULD YOU DO IF YOU FOUND YOURSELF IN A SIMILAR SITUATION?

WHAT WOULD YOU DO?

YOU GET GOOD GRADES IN EVERYTHING EXCEPT MUSIC. YET YOUR DREAM IS TO ROCK OUT ON THE GUITAR AND PERFORM YOUR OWN MUSIC SOMEDAY. YOUR FRIENDS AREN'T TOO SUPPORTIVE.

"A MUSICIAN?" SAYS ONE, "YOU CAN'T EVEN REMEMBER THE NAMES OF THE NOTES!"

MAYBE NOT, BUT YOU BELIEVE THIS IS SOMETHING YOU ARE MEANT TO DO. HOW COULD PERSEVERANCE HELP YOU IN ACHIEVING YOUR DREAM?

PERSEVERANCE AS TEACHER AND STUDENT

ANNE SULLIVAN AND HELEN KELLER

WHO ARE THEY?
A TEACHER AND HER STUDENT

WHY THEM?
ANNE SULLIVAN TAUGHT HER STUDENT, HELEN KELLER, TO COMMUNICATE WITH OTHERS—DESPITE THAT HELEN WAS BLIND AND DEAF.

HELEN KELLER ONCE SEEMED ALMOST UNTEACHABLE, BUT ANNE SULLIVAN NEVER GAVE UP ON HER.

LET'S SEE HOW BOTH TEACHER AND STUDENT PERSEVERED TO ACCOMPLISH MORE THAN ANYONE THOUGHT THEY WOULD.

IN HER YOUTH, ANNE HAD UNDERGONE MANY SURGERIES TO REPAIR HER FAILING EYESIGHT. SHE WORKED HARD AT THE PERKINS INSTITUTION AND MASSACHUSETTS SCHOOL FOR THE BLIND. WHEN SHE WAS JUST 19, THE SCHOOL RECEIVED A LETTER THAT WOULD CHANGE HER LIFE.

ANNE, THIS FAMILY HAS A DAUGHTER WHO IS BLIND AND DEAF. THEY DESPERATELY NEED HELP. WILL YOU BECOME A TEACHER FOR LITTLE HELEN KELLER?

IF YOU THINK I'M READY, THEN YES—I WILL GO GLADLY.

IN MARCH OF 1887, ANNE SULLIVAN ARRIVED AT THE KELLER RESIDENCE IN TUSCUMBIA, ALABAMA. SHE DIDN'T KNOW WHAT TO EXPECT...

THANK YOU FOR COMING, MISS SULLIVAN. WE JUST CAN'T SEEM TO REACH HELEN. SHE'S ALWAYS SO ANGRY. WE HOPE YOU CAN HELP HER.

THAT IS WHAT I HAVE COME TO DO, MR. KELLER.

18

A DOLL! WHAT A LOVELY GIFT!

WHAT ARE YOU DOING WITH HER HAND?

THIS IS CALLED **FINGER SPELLING.** I AM SPELLING THE WORD "DOLL." I WANT HELEN TO UNDERSTAND THAT EVERYTHING HAS A NAME.

BUT HELEN DIDN'T UNDERSTAND.

I'M SO SORRY, MISS SULLIVAN. I KNOW WE HAVEN'T BEEN FIRM ENOUGH WITH HELEN.

ANNE QUICKLY FOUND OUT THAT WITHOUT GUIDANCE, HELEN ACTED MORE LIKE A WILD ANIMAL THAN A LITTLE GIRL.

OH, HELEN, HOW CAN I TEACH YOU WORDS WHEN I CAN'T EVEN GET YOU TO BUTTON YOUR CLOTHES OR BRUSH YOUR HAIR?

I'D LIKE YOUR PERMISSION TO LIVE ALONE WITH HELEN IN YOUR LITTLE COTTAGE FOR A FEW DAYS. SHE HAS TO LEARN TO OBEY ME, OTHERWISE, I'LL NEVER BE ABLE TO TEACH HER.

DO YOU REALLY THINK...

YOU HAVE OUR PERMISSION, MISS SULLIVAN.

ANNE, LOOK! SHE UNDERSTANDS. SHE UNDERSTANDS!

HELEN LATER WROTE ABOUT THAT DAY, SAYING, "I LEFT THE WELL-HOUSE EAGER TO LEARN. EVERYTHING HAD A NAME, AND EACH NAME GAVE BIRTH TO A NEW THOUGHT."

YES! YES! OH, HELEN!

B-O-O-K

B-O-O-K!

IF IT HADN'T BEEN FOR ANNE'S PERSEVERANCE, HELEN KELLER MIGHT NEVER HAVE ESCAPED FROM HER DARK, SOUNDLESS WORLD. INSTEAD, SHE WENT TO COLLEGE, WROTE SEVERAL BOOKS, AND TRAVELED THE WORLD.

ANNE COULD HAVE GIVEN UP ON HELEN, BUT SHE DIDN'T! WHAT WOULD YOU DO IF YOU WERE IN A SIMILAR SITUATION?

WHAT WOULD YOU DO?

IMAGINE THAT YOU HAVE BEEN ASKED TO HELP A CLASSMATE WHO'S NEW TO THE SCHOOL AND IS HAVING TROUBLE FITTING IN. YOU MAKE MANY ATTEMPTS TO HELP HIM, BUT NO MATTER WHAT YOU DO, HE DOESN'T RESPOND. IN FACT, HE TELLS YOU TO JUST LEAVE HIM ALONE.

HOW COULD YOU PERSEVERE AND HELP YOUR CLASSMATE ADJUST TO HIS NEW SCHOOL?

PERSEVERANCE TO OVERCOME DISEASE

WILMA RUDOLPH

WHO IS SHE?
POLIO SURVIVOR AND OLYMPIC RUNNER

WHY HER?
SHE OVERCAME A *CRIPPLING* DISEASE TO BECOME A CHAMPION ATHLETE.

WILMA RUDOLPH DEVELOPED POLIO AS A YOUNG CHILD. SHE COULD HAVE SPENT HER LIFE IN LEG BRACES, BUT SHE DIDN'T! LET'S FIND OUT HOW HER PERSEVERANCE—AND THAT OF HER FAMILY—HELPED HER ACHIEVE HER DREAMS.

WILMA RUDOLPH WAS THE **20**TH CHILD BORN TO POOR BUT HARD-WORKING PARENTS. SHE WAS A SICK BABY, BUT THERE WERE MANY LOVING HANDS TO CARE FOR HER AT HOME.

MAMA, CAN I FEED BABY WILMA THIS TIME?

YOU SURE CAN! THANK YOU FOR THE HELP!

AS WILMA GREW, SHE FELL VICTIM TO POLIO—A CRIPPLING DISEASE WITHOUT A CURE. THE DOCTOR SAID WILMA WOULD NEVER WALK.

DON'T YOU WORRY ABOUT WHAT THAT DOCTOR SAID, WILMA. YOU WON'T JUST WALK—YOU'LL RUN!

AND SKIP AND JUMP, TOO!

Y AGE EIGHT, WILMA HAD
EARNED TO WALK WITH THE
ELP OF A METAL LEG BRACE
ND CRUTCHES. BUT HER FAMILY
OULDN'T LET HER STOP THERE.

SHOOT, WILMA!
YOU CAN DO IT!

I KNOW
I CAN!

THROUGH HARD WORK AND
PERSEVERANCE, WILMA BEAT AN
UNBEATABLE DISEASE. AND SHE COULD
DO A LOT MORE THAN JUST WALK...

WHAT A GAME!
WITH THAT LAST SHOT BY WILMA
RUDOLPH, BURT HIGH HAS EARNED
A SPOT IN THE TENNESSEE
STATE FINALS!

ONE DAY, A COACH FOR THE TENNESSEE
TIGERBELLES TRACK TEAM ASKED WILMA
TO JOIN HIS TEAM. SHE TRAINED FOR
HOURS EVERY DAY.

WILMA, YOUR TIMES ARE
OUTSTANDING. I THINK YOU
SHOULD TRY OUT FOR THE
OLYMPIC TRACK TEAM!

REALLY? DO YOU
REALLY THINK I
COULD QUALIFY?

THE WAY
YOU WORK?
I KNOW IT!

WILMA'S COACH CERTAINLY KNEW WHAT
HE WAS TALKING ABOUT! AFTER MONTHS
OF *INTENSE* TRAINING...

YOU DID IT!
WILMA YOU MADE
THE OLYMPIC TEAM

23

AND SHE DIDN'T. WILMA WON GOLD IN THREE EVENTS—THE 100M DASH, THE 200M DASH, AND THE 400M RELAY!

AMAZING RACE, WILMA! OUTSTANDING!

WILMA RUDOLPH BECAME THE FIRST AMERICAN WOMAN TO WIN THREE GOLD MEDALS AT THE SAME OLYMPICS. SHE WAS AN AMERICAN HERO AND AN INTERNATIONAL SUPERSTAR!

GOLD MEDAL—WILMA RUDOLPH, UNITED STATES OF AMERICA.

WHAT A STORY! BY REFUSING TO ACCEPT A FRIGHTENING *DIAGNOSIS*, WILMA'S FAMILY TAUGHT HER THE IMPORTANCE OF NEVER GIVING UP. THAT LESSON IN PERSEVERANCE TURNED HER INTO A CHAMPION.

IF YOU FACED DIFFICULTIES LIKE THESE, WHAT DO YOU THINK YOU WOULD DO?

WHAT WOULD YOU DO?

IMAGINE THAT YOU ARE PART OF THE DRAMA CLUB AT SCHOOL. A BLIND FRIEND LOVES TO ACT, BUT FEELS NERVOUS ABOUT TRYING OUT.

"WHAT'S STOPPING YOU?" YOU ASK.

"WHY SHOULD I THINK I COULD DO SOMETHING LIKE THIS," HE ANSWERS. "I MEAN, HOW MANY BLIND ACTORS DO YOU KNOW?"

WHAT WOULD YOU SAY TO GIVE YOUR FRIEND THE COURAGE TO PERSEVERE AGAINST THE ODDS?

THOMAS ALVA EDISON

WHO IS HE?
SCIENTIST AND INVENTOR

WHY HIM?
HE TRIED TO CREATE A LONG-LASTING LIGHT BULB POWERED BY ELECTRICITY.

> EDISON WAS ONE OF THE WORLD'S GREATEST INVENTORS. WHEN HE SET HIS MIND ON A GOAL OR HAD A PROBLEM TO SOLVE, HE NEVER GAVE UP—EVEN WHEN PEOPLE WERE SURE HE WOULD FAIL. LET'S SEE HOW EDISON'S PERSEVERANCE BROUGHT EVERYONE INTO A NEW AGE.

AS A YOUNG BOY, THOMAS EDISON LOVED EXPERIMENTS.

> I WONDER WHAT WOULD HAPPEN IF I TRIED TO HATCH AN EGG...

HIS EXPERIMENT FAILED WHEN HE BROKE THE EGG!

AS AN ADULT, EDISON CONDUCTED MORE **SOPHISTICATED** EXPERIMENTS. THEY OFTEN FAILED, BUT HE NEVER WANTED TO QUIT BEFORE FINDING A SOLUTION.

ATLANTIC & PACIFIC TELEGRAPH COMPANY

> SIR, I DON'T KNOW WHY I CAN'T GET THE TWO-WAY MESSAGE SYSTEM TO WORK. BUT IF YOU GIVE ME A LITTLE MORE TIME AND MONEY...

> I'M AFRAID WE ARE OUT OF BOTH, MR. EDISON. GOOD DAY, AND GOOD LUCK.

IT TOOK LONGER THAN HE ANTICIPATED, BUT IN 1879, THOMAS EDISON CREATED AN ELECTRIC LIGHT BULB THAT SUPPLIED CLEAR, STEADY LIGHT FOR 15 HOURS STRAIGHT. EDISON HAD ACCOMPLISHED WHAT HE SET OUT TO DO!

MAMA—IT LOOKS LIKE DAY OUT HERE!

IT'S WONDERFUL, SIMPLY WONDERFUL!

THOMAS EDISON CHANGED OUR WORLD THROUGH HARD WORK AND DETERMINATION. HIS PERSEVERANCE GAVE THE WORLD THE GIFT OF CLEAR, STEADY, ELECTRIC LIGHT. THINK ABOUT HIM THE NEXT TIME YOU SWITCH ON A LAMP AT HOME!

WHAT WOULD YOU DO?

YOU'RE WORKING ON A PROJECT FOR YOUR SCHOOL SCIENCE FAIR. YOUR GOAL IS TO CREATE A SMALL ROBOT THAT YOU CAN GUIDE WITH A REMOTE CONTROL.

AFTER SEVERAL ATTEMPTS, YOU CAN'T GET YOUR ROBOT TO WORK. IT WILL MOVE BACKWARD BUT NOT FORWARD! WHAT WOULD YOU DO? WHERE COULD YOU FIND HELP?

WEB SITEs

THIS WEB SITE FEATURES A COLLECTION OF STORIES ABOUT PEOPLE WHO ARE HEROES FOR THINGS THEY HAVE ACCOMPLISHED, DISCOVERED, CREATED, OVERCOME, AND INSPIRED.

www.myhero.com/myhero/home.asp

"LIFE ROLLS ON" IS A SITE DEDICATED TO PROVIDING HOPE FOR THOSE WHO PERSEVERE THROUGH LIFE—CHANGING SPINAL CORD INJURIES.

www.liferollson.org

THIS SITE CONTAINS PROFILES OF ATHLETES WHO HAVE RECEIVED THE AMATEUR ATHLETIC UNION'S TOP AWARD FOR MORAL CHARACTER. WILMA RUDOLPH WON THIS AWARD IN 1961.

www.aausullivan.org

FIND COOL INFORMATION ABOUT INVENTIONS AND INVENTORS AT ENCHANTED LEARNING.

www.enchantedlearning.com/inventors

LEARN ABOUT BRAILLE—AND A LOT MORE—AT BRAILLE BUG, SPONSORED BY THE AMERICAN FOUNDATION FOR THE BLIND.

www.afb.org/braillebug

VISIT THIS INTERESTING SITE FULL OF FACTS ABOUT THE TITANIC.

www.titanic-facts.com/titanic-facts.html

GLOSSARY

ARC LIGHTS LAMPS THAT PROJECT A STREAK OF BRIGHT LIGHT FOR A SHORT PERIOD OF TIME

BOILER FURNACE THE CONTAINER WHERE COAL IS BURNED FOR FUEL

CRIPPLING AFFECTING SOMEONE'S ABILITY TO MOVE

DEBRIS SCATTERED REMAINS, SUCH AS METAL OR WOOD

DIAGNOSIS IDENTIFYING A DISEASE OR ILLNESS THROUGH MEDICAL TESTING

ELECTRIC CURRENTS ELECTRICITY THAT MOVES IN A STREAM, OFTEN THROUGH A WIRE

ESPY AN AWARD GIVEN YEARLY TO INDIVIDUALS OR TEAMS THAT SHOW EXCELLENCE IN SPORTS PERFORMANCE

EXPEDITION A VOYAGE OR LONG JOURNEY

FILAMENT A FINE WIRE OR THREAD INSIDE A LIGHT BULB

FINGER SPELLING USING FINGERS TO PRESS SYMBOLS INTO THE PALM OF A BLIND AND DEAF PERSON'S HAND TO EXPLAIN WHAT OBJECTS ARE CALLED

FORESTER A PERSON WHO TAKES CARE OF FORESTS

FULL-ON A SURFING TERM FOR "EXCELLENT"

GNARLY A SURFING TERM FOR "AMAZING"

INCANDESCENT LIGHT ELECTRIC LIGHT THAT IS GLOWING AND BRIGHT

INSPIRATIONAL HAVING A POSITIVE INFLUENCE ON OTHERS

INTENSE SOMETHING STRONG OR DIFFICULT

INTERNATIONAL AMONG DIFFERENT COUNTRIES OF THE WORLD

LAMPBLACK BLACK SOOT FORMED BY BURNING OILS; USED LONG AGO TO MAKE BLACK PAINTS AND INK

MARINE GEOLOGIST SOMEONE WHO STUDIES THE OCEAN FLOOR AND COASTLINES

OPPORTUNITIES CHANCES TO DO SOMETHING SPECIAL

POLIO A DISEASE IN WHICH A PERSON'S SPINAL CORD BECOMES SWOLLEN AND PARTS OF THE PERSON'S BODY ARE NO LONGER ABLE TO MOVE

QUEST AN ADVENTUROUS SEARCH OR HUNT FOR SOMETHING

SOPHISTICATED SOMETHING THAT IS DETAILED AND COMPLICATED, SUCH AS SPECIAL EQUIPMENT

SYMBOLS SIGNS, LETTERS, PICTURES, OR ACTIONS THAT STAND FOR SOMETHING ELSE

TRANSMITTING SENDING OUT SIGNALS THROUGH ELECTRIC WAVES

WRECKAGE THE REMAINS OF SOMETHING THAT HAS BEEN DESTROYED

INDEX